Copper Thoughts

Copper Thoughts

The Copper Bell Poet

Foreword by Dr. J.B. Whitaker

Redwood Mountain Publishing

Contents

Dedication viii

FOREWORD 1

1 Fruits and Faults 3

2 A Flower in the Snow 5

3 Good Person 7

4 Pretend Evil 9

5 Society's Media 11

6 Productivity 13

7 Gravity 14

8 Matter 15

9 And The Whole World Can Dance on My Grave 16

10 A Brave New World 18

11 Fate 20

12 Past Bipolar 21

13 The Mocking Voice 22

Contents

14 Existential Eternity 24

15 "Solutions" 25

16 They, Me 26

17 Little Heart on the Shelf 27

18 Picture Frame 28

19 Colors 30

20 Rain 32

About The Author 33

Copyright © 2022 by Redwood Mountain Publishing

All rights reserved. This book or any portion thereof may not be reproduced or used in any manner whatsoever without the express written permission of the publisher except for the use of brief quotations in a book review or scholarly journal.

First Printing: 2022

Print ISBN 978-0-578-39863-1
eBook EISBN 978-0-578-39864-8

Redwood Mountain Publishing
1060 E 200 S Unit 302
Brigham City, UT 84302

Visit the Redwood Mountain Publishing website using the QR code below. You may subscribe to our mailing list to be notified of upcoming releases.

To young men and women everywhere.

Think big thoughts. Dream big dreams.

FOREWORD

THE COPPER BELL POET

The Copper Bell Poet has a gift for expressing herself through poetry. This book is a gift and I am encouraged that she has decided to share her talents. I believe strongly that such clever and powerful words should be illuminated for the whole world to feel.

The Copper Bell Poet was diagnosed with bipolar disorder at the age of ten. Accustomed to academic research, her father rummaged through the medical journals to see what the brightest minds had written about such a diagnosis in children. There was surprisingly little, but she needed something. The doctors seemed to know what they were doing, but it was a process of trial and error for her father. He closely monitored her behavior as she started a treatment regimen that included psychotherapy and medication.

At first her father was afraid the medication would dull the sassy creativity that he had come to love in her. She had been in trouble at school, but it was trouble born of a curious mind rather than any malevolent intent. She did things to see if she could, not to be unkind. For example, in second grade she hacked into a fellow student's email and sent a note to the teacher from this poor girl's account. The email called out several kids for their poor behavior and even referenced the Copper Bell Poet herself to throw the school authorities off her trail. She meant no harm to this girl and they remained friends after a heartfelt apology, but the allure of the clandestine act could not be passed up.

As she began her therapeutic journey, she and her father were amazed at how little her personality changed, but how much her awareness grew. She was able to articulate with great clarity how she was feeling. She developed the ability to read her own emotions and take steps to maintain, or quickly regain, her composure. Just as a bodybuilder strains against the weights to produce an extraordinary physique, the Copper Bell Poet's struggles produced an extraordinary inner balance that is enviable and worthy of emulation.

You will see revealed in some of the poems her struggle to find balance between the light and dark that she felt within, a light and dark she also observed in the world around her.

Despite her young age, the Copper Bell Poet thought big, deep thoughts. Her poems have caused me to reflect on the joys and sorrows of the human experience. Those who read her poetry will find themselves grasping at the deepest parts of their consciousness to try and comprehend the wisdom that they sense is there among the words, but perhaps not immediately accessible to the mind. I find a familiarity in her words, almost as if the thoughts were my own, that she somehow discovered them just for me.

The poems in this collection were authored by the Copper Bell Poet between the ages of ten and twelve. If a picture paints a thousand words, with one poem the Copper Bell Poet paints a thousand images that impose themselves suddenly and without warning on the mind's eye. The Copper Bell Poet is an inspiration to me and can be to others, especially those youth who may question their own value or worth. I hope you enjoy her poems as much as I do.

-J.B. Whitaker

{ 1 }

Fruits and Faults

The fault of your labor
The fruit of your labor
Absence and prosperity

Driving down a road I see on the side
A broken piece of wood and bristles
That bring an image to mind

Working, working
With such little pay
Saving every penny
For us, tucked away

Sweeping, sweeping
All night and day
Sweeping, sweeping
He swept his life away

No fun, no flare, no extra time
Not for us, not for him
Not to rest when he was tired
How many hours worked away

THE COPPER BELL POET

From nothing to little more?

We lived on what he'd saved
Enough for me to go to college,
Get a job and find a wife,
With our own two little children
No worries, no strife

Driving down the freeway
I see that splintered, broken broom
And promise my family that,
Though I work for them,
I'll be there for them too

{ 2 }

A Flower in the Snow

Have hope and you will fly.
Your tears heal others as you cry;
They'll know it's not enough to try.

Stand with others and you will shine.
Perhaps it should change our pace of mind.

Don't point out they've fallen down.
Stand them up so they can see
What pushed them to the ground.

Sing until you learn to grow,
Like a flower in the snow.

But ponder this as you sing:
Without the silver white,
Would the pastels and green gleam?

Is one stubborn and rude,
Unwilling to wait its turn to shine?
The next pushing all other beauty down,
Taking the ground and saying "It's mine?"

THE COPPER BELL POET

The extravagant flower or the glistening snow?
The answer is neither, without both.

{ 3 }

Good Person

You give gratitude and help others in need,
Have a positive attitude and push away greed.

You apologize, not lie.
You are trustworthy in many eyes.

You speak your mind (if the thoughts are kind).
If someone is hurt you stand by their side
Even if that means you get left behind.

You don't look down on people who do wrong,
Always empathizing, forgiving,
And helping them feel like they belong.

Does a single one of these traits fit you and your mind?
Aren't you this person? Loving and kind?

Because you can be!

If you've read this,
You've been taught!
So if you say "I can't!"

THE COPPER BELL POET

There's no good answer to the question: why not?

{ 4 }

Pretend Evil

I traded my life to the TV.
My sight and heart belong online
To videos, characters and games.

They say it's bad, that I should stop;
"These things, they don't mean anything."
They don't understand that that's just it!
In that world it's all pretend.
Evil scenarios people make,
Bad things people say,
They might not *mean* in real life.
Everything's pretend behind a screen.

I think I like the trade I made.
I'll keep my fake reality
Where everything means nothing
So nothing is truly bad.

I'd rather be here,
I'd rather hear,
I'd rather see,
Evil things where it's a *good* thing

THE COPPER BELL POET

To feel *anything*,
Than in real life
In Real Life.

{ 5 }

Society's Media

Doesn't Society's Media work in strange ways?
Blurring the lines of opinion and fact?

Makes you wonder, and (wrongly) accuse
And assume all happiness is an act.
A mask.
Nothing more than a trap.
Because sometimes, sadly,
Kindness is used simply as that.

The Media twists and turns,
So much that everyone hates it.
Yet, no one has, would, or will,
Do anything to change it.

It's almost as if we want it,
To know we know we're wrong,
But we all still sing a willing song.

It pulls in anything,
Then everything washes up:
A great big pile of information

THE COPPER BELL POET

We know we don't want.
Like a title wave;
Informative, toxic,

Makes the world feel we should be ashamed.
We're brainwashing our brains.

Doesn't The Media work in odd ways?
Hiding the things we find,
Finding the things we hide.
Makes it so we can't trust anything
Because anything could be a lie.

The world (us) wants to hear
What we don't want to know.
So until (if ever) something changes,
That's how it'll go.

{ 6 }

Productivity

'When' is a Concept,
Indulgence: a Crime.
Wasting Hours,
Selling Seconds,
Forever Losing Time.

Giving Time to be content.
Time *will* pass by.
Not like you can save it.
It's a fair trade.
Why let it under your skin?

'When' is just a question and
Indulgence is a gift.

{ 7 }

Gravity

Gravity, it holds me down.
I don't fly off, and yet I frown.
Is it really better on the ground?

{ 8 }

Matter

I am made of matter; but does that mean I do?
It makes less sense when you think it through.
What matters to me might not matter to you.
But we're both made of matter so we must too!
You matter to me, do I matter to you?

{ 9 }

And The Whole World Can Dance on My Grave

Sing a sappy song
Then jump into the river.
Have to drown in my own thoughts
For the fish think I'm a swimmer.
My cliché mind: words instead of waves,
And the whole world can dance on my grave.

Castle stand wide,
Armor shine bright,
Protect the secrets locked inside.
Ask the difference of a knight and a knave,
And the whole world can dance on my grave.

Too mad to yell,
Too tired to sleep.
Too rich to sell,
Too sad to weep.
Wrong time, longer week.
Happy morning, worse day,
And the whole world can dance on my grave.

Copper Thoughts

Dance a happy beat
After the sorrow's chased away.
For grieving or for gladness:
A few may have a say.
The birds *may* sing,
But night will turn to day
And the whole world can dance on my grave.

A tombstone was strewn of tears,
Unsure why dusk did not appear.
I've lost all reason not to care.
It's better to become a slave!
You could buy the loss it feels to be saved,
And the whole world can dance on my grave.

{ 10 }

A Brave New World

A Brave New World
risen from ashes
With crimson eyes
and bloodstained lashes.
Alive and awakened by what they've seen.
Not ready to be one.
but determined to succeed.

A Brave New World
regifted and reborn.
Upset yet content,
by chaos it's sworn.
Each has their own purpose,
their own life to command.
Yet they all know they're all one
like a body of sand.

A Brave New World
that bickers and fights.
Like a wind through salt hail
on forever stormy nights.
It destroys itself because it knows

Copper Thoughts

it takes the worst for the best to show.

The best keep going

Until...

They do not,
now lost too, to this fight
that cannot be fought
with a victor.

{ 11 }

Fate

It doesn't matter that I'm mad
Or things will turn out for the worst.

It doesn't matter that I'm sad
Or although I feel I could just burst.

It doesn't matter that I can't think straight,
A broken hinge, a creaking gate.

It feels like I could crumble
And it feels like I could break
Underneath the everlasting weight of
A single thought,
A single thread,
Yet still enough to wind up dead.

A little light to seal your fate;
You've changed your mind but it's too late.

… { 12 }

Past Bipolar

PAST
People liked me better
After I got my meds
Still I feel I remain an ID card
Like I'm in debt for my creativity
To my present, not past

BIPOLAR
Bye my friends I bullied away.
I'm sorry I was so mean,
so unaware that others have their own spotlight.
Pretending I was nice in the past,
that all of it was this manic-depression,
is a lie.
Over and over I did crude, stupid things.
Lacking, completely, a sense of Empathy.
Always thinking only of myself.
I'm different, better now!
But
Review, rewind, and you will find
I might not be all that kind.

The Mocking Voice

Most times,
When I feel bad, frustrated,
I cry.

Sometimes,
When I feel bad,
I'll catch my reflection
In a mirror,
A window,
Sometimes even faintly on a table.

I don't say anything.
My reflection doesn't speak.
It's just a red-faced, watery-eyed me
Staring at a red-faced, watery-eyed me.

But,
There's something about my reflection.
Something in its eyes.
Something...
Fake.

Copper Thoughts

They seem to mock me, taunting:
Cry little baby!
Whine, kick, scream.
Cry your selfish tears of
"I can't"
Boo. Hoo.

You think you fool them?
Don't say you're not acting.
You think you fool *yourself*?

Ha!
They see right through
Your "pity me" panic.

They all get tired of dealing with your fits
Eventually.

Throw your tantrums,
Nothing's
Gonna
Change.

{ 14 }

Existential Eternity

I don't know why I'd stay,
I don't know why I'd go.
But I'll keep going this way
'til that way is home.

I don't know why I'd go,
I don't know why I'd stay.
But I'll keep waiting here
'til things go my way.

Then, Maybe,
I'll finally be free.

They're watching, it's unlikely, but at this point
Only innocence could ever frighten me.

{ 15 }

"Solutions"

Wouldn't be heard
Couldn't get in a word.

Knocked to the floor
Still I'm begging for more.

Hiding away
For the rest of the day.

Ignoring common sense
Using the easy "solution" instead.

I'll face my problems when they *urgently* come,
But for now I'm busy making bigger ones.

{ 16 }

They, Me

They
They Come,
They take,
They give,
But they never leave.
Their hearts are filled with pity,
But their minds are full of greed.

Me
Am I fun? Obnoxious?
Or maybe, I'm just crude.
I rarely win,
I always leave,
But I'll never lose.

{ 17 }

Little Heart on the Shelf

              Little heart up on the shelf.
                  Someday,
One day,
      Fun days
             Will come.

            Little heart up on the shelf.
                The dust dusted off
          And the cobwebs brushed away,

           Lonely heart upon the shelf.
               Taken down and
                Clean once more,
                Beat once more,
            Little heart on the shelf.

{ 18 }

Picture Frame

Like a painting in a picture frame,
Beautifully trapped to society's gaze.
With nowhere to go, no one to be,
Nothing to do, but let them see.

They see and point and "ooh" and "aah"
At what they all are told is passion.
The blame is un-retainable. It's unreasonable.

The seasons of old are shaking their heads
at the power we give again and again to thoughtless things like fashion.

Art is easy; it takes no direction,
You could draw a wobbly circle,
They'd believe it was perfection.

Rhyme a few words, call it a wonder. A poem!
They'd believe it if you told them.

Truth to be, it's more than that,
The unwilling eye can see.

Copper Thoughts

It takes passion and energy.

<u>Real art has meaning.</u>
It's something meant to represent.
It has something to be.

The world can judge, the world can think.
The world forgets what it believes.
Always assuming it's in the right,
It changes only to please,
Never stopping to think:
"Oh wait, *this applies to me.*"

{ 19 }

Colors

The world is not as black and white
As many people think.
In fact it's much more gray,
Say much more in between.

Oh, but the world is not so bleak,
Not so full of hopelessness
Not so full of whining.
Nay, this world is chock full
Of shiny silver linings.

Merely silver? Ha!
Not everything has equal value.
This world is of gold, silver, bronze,
Iron, and others, merely flowers.

No! No! Cried another.
We're not all in competition!
Yes, it's true that there are differences,
But they should be loved!
We should be lovers!
This world is a rainbow full of color.

Copper Thoughts

Each as beautiful as the next,
None greater than another.

And so the world bickered and pleaded and puzzled
Over something as earthy as the world's own colors.
What about its smells?
What about its tastes?
Why must we label
What will differ and change?

Rain

I don't mind feeling empty
I just don't want to feel dull
And the thought of feeling average
Seems worse than feeling full

I do not crave purpose
I do not crave joy
Not excitement, nor peace, but pain

I need motivation, not meaning
Wind through hilltops, not bells ringing

Not a song, nor a dance
Not even to be okay
What I truly need to feel
Is Rain

THE COPPER BELL POET

The Copper Bell Poet has struggled with anxiety and manic-depression for nearly all of her life. It was like she had been wandering around a dark room in her mind, hurting herself by falling over things, hitting the floor and getting back up, then stubbing her foot, scraping her arm, or hitting her shin, until she just kicked and stomped everything out of her way. Rampaging through the darkness and splintering any objects in her way. Then one day she stopped. She stopped because she realized that every time she smashed or stomped or kicked something it hurt just as much as falling over it and the splintered and shattered pieces were making it increasingly dangerous to walk around anymore.

So...she stopped and stood there. Blind. She hated this darkness coating her while she silently stood still and wanted to move so badly, but knew too well that if she took so much as a step she would trip or fall onto the broken things. So she stood there in utter, crushing, defeat. "Standing in the dark forever," she thought.

But, she did not stand in the dark forever. She put her hands out and attempted to stretch her tired limbs and felt a wall. She didn't know this at the time, but that wall had been put there, brick by brick, from the outside, by her friends and family and therapist and teachers. Feeling this wall was such a shock to her after feeling nothing but air for so long, and nothing but broken sharp bits before that, and before that nothing but hard floor and shapes hitting her shins.

It shocked her so much that she took a step forward. Then another. Then another. Slowly she felt her way around the room until she wasn't holding on to the brick wall anymore; it was her own wall. She kept feeling and stepping over shapes on the floor until she felt something on the wall; a light switch. After flipping it, lights came on very slowly, bit by bit until...she could see!

What she saw was not a pretty sight. It was the shattered toys, the broken furniture, and the smashed photos that she had broken in her stumbling. She was distressed and frustrated. She wanted to smash herself into bits for everything. She could see now, everything she could do and everything she had done, and she loathed everything about it, and yet, she could see. So she walked around without having to worry about stepping or tripping over things for a while and then began to clean up. "This...is useful" she decided, "and...beautiful."

After getting used to seeing in this little house in her mind she looked out the window for the first time. She saw a whole world in her head for her to explore and understand and other people's houses that she could try and see into. She saw worlds to explore with flowers like ice and skies like mountains and mountains like rivers, a wonderful place where you could learn anything from nothing and make something happen, explore impossible things, and comprehend the incomprehensible, with new things always flowing in from real life to be tinkered and tested and turned inside out! Then she was outside, input, into "real life."

"I have to show everyone my world" she thought, but there was no picture she could take with her and words got all jumbled in her mouth. So, she picked up a pencil.

www.ingramcontent.com/pod-product-compliance
Lightning Source LLC
Chambersburg PA
CBHW071846290426
44109CB00017B/1949